Shipping Container Homes

The Step-By-Step Guide to Shipping Container Homes and Tiny house living, Including Examples of Plans and Designs

Contents

INTRODUCTION – WHY SHIPPING CONTAINERS? 7

CHAPTER 1 – THE GOOD AND BAD 11

THE GOOD 13
Cost 13
The Time 15
Eco Considerations 16
Safer and Stronger 18
THE BAD 19
It's Steel 19
Contaminants 20
Weatherproofing 21

CHAPTER 2 – DESIGNING YOUR HOME....23

PREFABRICATED 23
PLANS 25
BUILDING CODES 28
Zoning 30
Where Not to look at Property 34
PURCHASING LAND 35
Property Access Rights 36

Water..37

Resources 39

Pollution, Utilities, and Easements............40

Legal Protection..41

CHAPTER 3 – YOUR CONTAINERS...............44

INSPECTING THE CONTAINER 45

WHERE TO PURCHASE 47

Online..47

Direct..48

COST...49

CHAPTER 4 – PREPARING THE LAND........51

FOUNDATIONS 51

Concrete Piers..52

Slab-on-Grade..53

Pile Foundation 54

Strip Foundation..55

CONCRETE...55

Footings..58

Fixing the Container 62

CHAPTER 5 – CRAFTING THE CONTAINER
....64

CONNECTING CONTAINERS..64

Stacking, Clustering or Both 65

INTERIOR CONSIDERATIONS 70

Side Wall Modification....................................70

Windows and Doors..72

CHAPTER 6 – INSULATION 78

FRAMING THE CONTAINER 79
Fiberglass *79*
Foam *81*
Panel Insulation *83*
Blanket Insulation *83*
LIVING ROOF 84

CONCLUSION **87**

PREVIEW OF AN ESSENTIAL GUIDE TO SHIPPING CONTAINER HOMES WITH EXAMPLES AND IDEAS OF DESIGNS ... 123

Introduction – Why Shipping Containers?

When it comes to re-purposing, the 21st century has become a time of reusing and recycling just about anything. Most people and corporations are becoming more concerned about their impact on the planet since the human race has managed to violently destroy so much of it in so little time. When we look at the span of human existence we're merely a blip in the timeline, yet in that time pollution, deforestation, oil exploitation and many other industrial processes have killed off numerous species and rendered huge areas as polluted or useless for anything but industrial purpose.

While shoes are made from recycled soda bottles, and cans into solar heaters, commercial shipping containers remain one of the largest sources of recycled steel. The containers are nothing more than giant corrugated steel boxes which fit together like building blocks, and it's this concept that has made them into the ideal "tiny home". That's not saying that all container homes are tiny, in fact many modernist designs use as many as 50+ containers in behemoth designs. But is there really any advantage to them? Sure, it's recycling but wouldn't the steel be better used elsewhere?

The trend to make these boxes into homes has been a concept that's been used for almost two decades now. The idea peaked about 5 years ago, and since then they've been a convenient design concept that works well with the tiny home movement. The idea of minimizing and having pre-made deliverable homes that fit easily onto the back of a standard truck has a lot of appeal. There's a lot of flexibility when it comes to designing one of these homes, whether you're going for the tiny home or a unique modern design concept.

There are two main types of containers that can be used to make homes, but the most common is a simple Dry Freight container that has front facing doors and a sealed end. Tank containers come in a cylinder shape and while these are less common the unique round sides have a certain appeal, especially for someone putting together a modular design. Asides from these two you can also find open topped hoppers and various thermal and refrigeration units, but because of the shape these are often too small and difficult to work with to create enough space inside.

Modular design has a lot of appeal, it means the homes can be created and moved without much difficulty, even shipped elsewhere fully finished. The small footprint also means they're much easier to transport than traditional modular designs which must be broken down before being put in their final location, and which then can't be moved, unlike a shipping container. In fact, in shape and size these are very similar to most trailer homes, though more sturdy.

The demand for housing, especially in urban areas, has skyrocketed in the past couple of decades and being able to produce living space that's not only functional but fits into ever shrinking space has a lot of appeal. In fact, one of the design concepts we will look at further on shows a building where your shipping container home could simply be slotted in and out of a building anywhere in the world. Especially in developing nations being able to deliver housing, classrooms, or even work areas readymade and fitted out without incurring huge building costs makes sense. Pre-fabricated housing has been around for almost a century and it's been shown to be especially advantageous for places where housing is scarce or too expensive.

Home ownership is getting harder and harder, and it's not just in the developed world. Even small homes are worth a fortune. Just recently a house in London sold for £700,000 and it was a mere 290 square feet. That's the size of the average living room, and it sold for almost a quarter million just because it was in Chelsea despite needing to be completely renovated. The average shipping container costs a lot less than that and even when it's fully fitted out it's far cheaper.

Still not convinced?

Even though shipping container homes are my favorite homes and buildings, it's important to note that they are not for everyone. Read on to see just what the good and bad are to help you make that decision.

Chapter 1 – The Good and Bad

No matter how you look at it there are pros and cons of owning and building any type of home. Whether you're looking at traditional brick architecture, a rustic log cabin or a modern shipping container house there's reasons that you have to take into account before jumping in. Shipping container homes might be modern and trendy but you could end up sinking money into a design you hate or spending far more than you anticipated before you can even move in.

The first thing you need to consider is whether you're going for the "tiny home" concept using a single container or one of the larger designs which stacks or connects multiple units together to create a larger living space. Shipping containers are a standard 40' long but you can also get 45' high cube containers too or small 20' mini containers. While the 20' will be much too small except as an addition, the average size is about 2377 cubic feet for a regular container and 3026 cubic feet for a high cube. Now, taking into account the fact that you've got to insulate it and add pipes etc under the floor, the high cube container only has a maximum height of 8'10" so you're going to have a short ceiling for a single unit. Unless you're stacking the standard container or the small 20' containers you're not going to have enough height for a single home, but they can be convenient "building blocks" to add to a modular concept home.

The Good

Cost

Most shipping container homes cost less than standard housing. Part of the reason behind this is the size, they're much smaller than most duplexes or apartments, but they're still self contained. Creating a home the same size from standard materials would cost almost double in comparison to simply repurposing a container. The average used container costs less than $5000 and some actually already come with kits or designs ready for customization. A smaller 20' container costs as little as $1400.Meanwhile you can actually buy brand new containers for only a little more than this.

On top of the container itself you'll need to insulate it. Insulation is especially important otherwise the container will turn into an oven in the summer and be too cold in the winter. There are three options with insulation with the cheapest being about $0.30/ft². The outside of the home will also need some sort of cladding if you don't want it to look like a shipping container. While this might seem to defeat the point some people do want their home to look like a home, and in some areas zoning requirements state that the homes have to be camouflaged to blend in to the local area. You can expect to pay $2-3 per square foot of this.

You'll also need to factor in laying a basic foundation for the home to stand on. This will stop the home sitting in wet ground and provide a level platform. Concrete itself is also fairly inexpensive and there are three different techniques that can be used. The cheapest foundation for a 40' container is about $550, and while it's not the most attractive or sturdy if the bottom line is where your thoughts are at it will do the job.

These are just the basics, you're not factoring in appliances or fitted features.

The average container home costs just $35,000 to build not including the land but can be as much as $50,000 or more if you're going for a structure made of multiple containers. Most homes that are in desirable areas do not cost even close to this. In fact, while you'll see foreclosed homes in poor or dangerous neighborhoods for less, if you want a modern and well designed house you won't get anything close in price. Purchasing one that's already fitted out will cost you close to the base price of some small houses, but since you've got the option for customization it's more like building a home that costs 2-3 times as much.

The Time

Did you know that a shipping container home can be finished in days? If you're not simply ordering something that has already been completed elsewhere a simple home can take less than a week for competent builders to put together. Most homes take months or even years to complete depending on the design. While this is a professional turnaround you can still expect to complete the design quicker than a standard house if you're doing it yourself, plus you aren't forced to hire licensed builders, architects, or surveyors because you're not actually building anything.

While most of us want to get into our new home quickly, being able to go from a box to move-in ready in less than a week is impressive. Most people don't even manage to move into an apartment that fast. For those that like the idea of being able to move, a shipping container home is also portable since it can be designed to go onto a truck and put down anywhere in the world as long as the hook-ups and foundation is there. If you were to pack up your traditional home you would have to unpack, and find a new place that you may not like as well. This way you keep your home, exactly as you like it. There's actually a similar concept that's used for promotions where the office/hub is simply boxed back up and shipped wherever the company wants it, saving time and money.

Eco Considerations

This is a rather gray area, as some people consider the shipping homes to be a great method of recycling defunct containers, while others bemoan the fact that this is the largest source of recycled steel and therefore taking away a resource better used elsewhere. There is a huge abundance of abandoned or unused containers, especially in coastal regions. A lot of the time it's simply cheaper for companies to ship containers filled with goods and just leave the container at the destination. Shipping the empty container back costs more than simply getting a new one again at the original port. At any time there are thousands of disused containers sitting around which means there are plenty of opportunities to purchase them. While many are simply melted down as recycled steel that process releases carbon and other industrial contaminants.

By re-purposing the container "as is" you're cutting out the carbon impact of recycling the material while still doing just that. Not only this but if you take into account the carbon impact of building a regular home or an apartment building instead of using the containers you'll also find the amount is significantly less. You're doubly keeping your carbon footprint down and stopping more contaminants, carbon, and waste happening by reusing the container.

The reason this is a gray area is that the recycled steel is actually needed. Many building and commercial processes need recycled steel to happen – for equipment, buildings, etc. And by taking away this source you're either forcing them to buy new steel (not environmentally friendly) or encouraging them to use different methods that may not be as eco-friendly.

Safer and Stronger

Have you ever watched a news video after a tornado has passed through? It's almost a guarantee you will see shipping containers tossed around like toys. But the one thing you can guarantee is that they still look like shipping containers, they're still recognizable, and while they may be battered they're not destroyed into matchsticks like the traditional timber framed houses around them. In areas where natural disaster can strike at any moment a shipping container is a much safer choice than traditional building. These containers are designed to stand up to battering sea winds and the harsh bumps of global transport. This makes them much safer.

A traditional timber frame home is surprisingly flimsy. In the last century the trend for building brick and mortar construction has dropped, since it takes so long to do and because it's not as economical to build. When profits are the bottom line getting a house up fast and passing codes is all that matters. Consider the fact that older homes often survive centuries and natural disasters while newer homes usually crumble under the first cyclone that passes through.

What about simple theft? A standard home has a lot of windows and doors, plus you can drive a car through the wall and there's a huge gaping hole. A shipping container is made of solid steel, it's not going to let you get in or out, and while you're probably going to put in windows and doors they're likely to be much smaller than those found in a standard home, making it a much more secure home.

The Bad

It's Steel

Steel isn't the primary building material in most homes for a reason – it rusts. Shipping containers were made for one purpose – to ship goods. They serve their life and are then recycled because usually they have become structurally compromised. This means that while ideally and in brand new condition they are safe and strong, as a used container they can be risky.

In their lifespan most containers get bumped about pretty significantly. They might get banged into, dinged up, dented, and scratched. Most people know that steel rusts when it's exposed to air and water, and especially seawater. Since these containers essentially live their entire lifetime near seawater there is a good chance that any used container has rust. Even if rust spots are painted over they compromise the structural integrity of the container, and will spread under the paint. If you want to deal with this, you have to sandblast the container and recoat it.

Contaminants

While you might think you're doing the world a favor and saving on contaminants and pollution by reusing the container how can you be sure what you're being exposed to? Most containers are used for industrial purposes and can be exposed to any number of chemicals, not least lead-based paint. In its lifetime that container could have been used once, or could have been used a hundred times to transport carcinogens, chemicals, toxins, biohazards, or something else.

Containers are built all over the world, and while there's a basic standard design the materials are not always created equal. One company may already be using recycled steel. You also don't know for sure what that container has been exposed to between it's construction that might have affected it's integrity. Steel is pretty strong, which is why it's used for skyscrapers, but it's vulnerable to extreme temperatures and, especially if the paint is scratched, could be impossible to clean of all contaminants. While creating your home you're going to have to drill into that steel which can release microparticles, and while you're living in it you could spend years being exposed to compounds that will cause you to get ill.

Weatherproofing

If you've ever picked up a metal or glass jar and put something cold inside it on a hot day then you know the outside of the container will start to sweat. Steel is a very good conductor meaning it transfers and holds heat well. This makes it incredibly hard to control the inside temperature of the container without an excessive amount of insulation. It's impossible to keep all the heat out of a container and it's difficult to keep heat in. The design is simply not made to work that way, unlike conventional construction which creates several barrier layers between you and the outside environment. One way that you can solve this is to make sure that the home gets the right insulation.

Chapter 2 – Designing Your Home

France has some of the most creative and innovative housing designs using shipping containers. While there are notable designs all over the world when it comes to actually creating a livable space it seems French Architects have this nailed. The simplest homes are nothing more than an insulated box, which means that there's very little design needed. This is especially true of prefabricated designs.

Prefabricated

A simple Google search will bring you up a number of companies offering pre-fab homes. These have any number of different designs and shapes and may or may not come with appliances. They average $21-40,000. The most notable company is Atomic Container Homes. Their designs range from simple boxy, stackable, units that look much like the site offices of large construction companies, to innovative and modern designs with windows and chic constructs. Atomic isn't cheap by any means, and that's because their homes are custom designed for you and you have 100% control over the design.

Ironically you can actually order these units on ebay. The company sells off designs that were either not popular with the client or that were made as samples. Some of them cost up to $300,000! The ebay designs are essentially pre-fab kits, container homes designed with everything you need that arrives ready to be put together and connected. This includes a diagram book, studs, and all the materials to create the design yourself and even includes scrap materials to practice the methods on so you'll get it right when you're actually building your container home. Their simplest kit costs a mere $17,895.

The company has been around for two decades now and is based out of Scottsdale Arizona. They have a team of architects and designers and their own construction company which does the installation for you. They have a dedicated factory in Texas which you can visit to see your home being built before it arrives. They use big brand companies like IKEA and 3M to insure quality. They also have their own finance team so you can set up a mortgage just like a regular house if you don't have the capital to buy outright. They also have options for off-grid bunkers, hurricane proofing, bullet-proofing, and three standard levels of build construction so you can decide how technical you want to get.

Buying a pre-fab container home is no different than buying a pre-fab regular home, you choose the company, one of their plans, and they build it for you on your land. It's the simplest way of owning a container home and takes the least effort. But it's also the most expensive.

Plans

The first step in creating your home is to design it. The design stage allows you to map out how you want your space to look and how it's put together. A simple one container home just needs you to figure out the space, windows, doors and hook ups, while a more complex design will require an architect. There are several companies that produce schematic designs for container homes. One of the best companies for this is ContainerPlans. Not only can they custom design you a plan but their pre-made design layouts can cost as little as $10 per schematic. These schematics will allow your construction crew, or your architect at least, to see what you want and where to put things.

Their plans are quite complex, but this is essential for showing just where everything will go. Unlike Atomic they don't include permits, any engineering work, and while the drafting is professional they are not architect or engineer designed so there's no guarantee that the concept will be viable.

Plans

Plan by Matt Brown

Here is an example of how you can design your shipping container home.

One 40ft Containers

Bedroom	Living	Kitchen	Bath-room

1 bedroom unit

One 40ft Container

Unit 1	Bath-room	Bath-room	Unit 2
	Door		Door

2 bedroom unit

Two 20ft Containers

Bedroom	Kitchen	Bath-room
Living room	Bedroom	

2 bedroom unit

Two 40ft Containers

Bedroom	Dining	Bedroom	
Bedroom	Living	Kitchen	Bath room

3 bedroom unit

The picture above also shows how you can arrange the containers as well as the inside of your home.

Photograph by Nicolás Boullosa
(https://www.flickr.com/photos/faircompanies/198154064 13)

Building Codes

Before you start building or buying anything you need to know what your local requirements are. This also includes land, you don't want to waste money buying a parcel of land only to find out it's not zoned residential and you're not allowed to put a shipping container design on it anyway because it's against neighborhood rules. This applies whether your design comes from a pre-fab kit or construction. The first place to go is the local government administration offices in the county where you plan to build. They will have a planning and zoning department which is responsible for permits. If you've been looking at certain land as a potential site take that information with you as well as any pictures or plans with the design you want. While it's likely you'll only need this if a hearing comes up, many people have not heard or seen shipping container homes and having examples which show them as a home and not an eyesore can really help. They will also be able to give you information about licenses and applications.

Before you start the local office may have some requirements, and these will also add to the final cost of your home. Things like soil tests, the requirement of easements from public land to where you're planning on putting your home, and whether you'll be able to rezone or not if your property isn't in an appropriate area. Fees differ county by county so there's not really a rough estimate that can be given of these extra costs.

Zoning

The first one you're going to encounter is zoning. Zoning is defined by the local council as what the land may be used for. You'll often see this on for sale boards as letters – zoned F, C, R etc. Just because the land is empty it doesn't mean that it can be built on in the way you want it. You will need pre-approval to build or the council can fine you and require you to move it at your cost.

If you've started looking at land think about what buildings are around it. Do you have any neighbors that may object? Will putting a container home affect property values around it? While some large homes made of multiple containers have a modern look that can be integrated with regular housing a design like the single container above may negatively affect property values and you're likely to get denied. Similarly, if you're planning on building in a remote or rural area the land may be zoned for agricultural and farming use only.

Finding out this information usually requires either searching the local administration office online database or going to talk to them in person. The building department will have everything you need to know about your location and permits. Zoning laws are complicated which is why you should double check in person with your requirements already set out.

Shipping container homes are not considered pre-feb manufactured homes and often have their own requirements, do not make the mistake of trying to fake your way through it using this term only to find that once you actually put it up it can't stay.

The reason zoning is a big deal is because the regulations allow for specific laws governing how far apart buildings need to be and how much space from the center of the road is actually owned by the government as an easement and not the property owner. These are known as Setbacks, and this differs based on the type of structure which is why something may not be able to be rezoned. Compliance with setback rules needs to be determined before any construction can begin and must include all sides of the property.

New York has some of the easiest to explain laws in this area. In the city residential areas are zoned R1-10. R1 zones are largest and have bigger lots which tend to be single family dwellings in more suburban or less populated brownstone districts. R10 zones are those with large apartment buildings or high-rises which are likely multi-family use. These are both residential zones and not commercial zones which means that any business that wants to set-up on this land or construction for business purposes must include permits and potential rezoning, even if the building itself stays the same outside and construction only takes place inside.

Checklist:

Before purchasing property make sure you have all the information that you'll need about what your home will look like and how it works. Bringing construction plans and designs can really help in this instance as many counties do not have explicit laws for shipping container homes and they may be outright denied because of preconceived notions that they will be an eyesore. The more information you can provide the more likely your permits are to be allowed as it shows you've spent time researching and that this is a serious build.

1. Start by calling your local building administration at the county offices then stop by in person with the plans to talk to someone about the type of building.
2. Consider multiple properties as rural areas are more likely to allow you to build alternative structures than residential neighborhoods which may have a financial impact. You can also canvas the neighborhood you're looking at and ask people if they're okay with you building there (with a preliminary design) and have them give you support in writing.
3. Before you purchase ask about the Parcel Identifier. The PID will confirm what sort of zoning the property has and whether it is suitable for you to build on. It will allow you to talk with the administration about whether you can have it rezoned or not and what covenants are on the property.
4. Ask about zones or laws that are specific to shipping container homes and not just pre-fabricated buildings. This will double-check that your shipping container is allowed and not just that construction of a home in general or a modular home is allowed. Do not be surprised if

there isn't a specific law in this instance but make sure you have confirmation in writing that the shipping container specifically is allowed.

5. Have the soil tested. If you're ready to purchase this is the last step as the soil quality can determine whether the land is suitable to hold the weight of the container and any other construction. Not all soil is suitable for building work and you may find that the area is a drainage swamp.

6. Do not buy any property until you know it is suited for your purposes and that the rules and regulations will work for shipping container construction. You may face large legal fees and lose money otherwise.

Where Not to look at Property

Not every location is suitable for shipping container construction. The reason for this is mostly climate based. Since the containers are hard to insulate choosing an especially hot or cold location is going to incur extra costs to make the project work. It goes without saying that choosing somewhere extremely cold would require both inside and outside insulation as well as less windows to keep the box warm. This means you may have a rather dark interior. Similarly, in a desert region you're going to pay an extortionate amount just trying to keep it cool in summer and daytime temperatures.

As a solution to developing countries basic shipping container homes are meant to be temporary for this reason, they can become totally inhabitable when the mercury rises too far.

Avoid properties that are too close to water unless you're planning on constructing some sort of platform. Steel rusts which means that any scrapes during construction or exposed steel could become vulnerable to rust. If the box is sitting on a flood plain then should that water level rise your home may end up inhabitable when the integrity of the trailer rusts away.

Purchasing Land

At this point you should know everything there is to know about the parcel of land you want, or do you? If you have chosen a rural location you'll need to look at a few things. Purchasing

Property Access Rights

You would think that buying rural land in the middle of nowhere would be easiest, but if your land isn't directly connected to the public throughway (road) how are you planning on getting to it? You have two choices – purchase land to get to/from your land and the road, or work out an easement that allows you to get back and forth over the land owned by someone else. Just because you have purchased and owned the rights to your land it doesn't mean you have the right to get to it through someone else. The best way of describing this is that your owned land is an island, and the "land" surrounding it is an ocean, without a boat or bridge you can't get to it and you need to either buy the bridge or rent the boat.

There are no legal means to force another landowner to give you access, and just because the previous owner used a certain path for years it does not mean they have to give you the same benefit. Accessing your land via another is called an easement, this gives you permission to use their land for a certain purpose without actually purchasing it and may come with additional conditions like maintaining the road, or keeping the hedges trimmed at your cost. This MUST be in writing, or at any time the landowner can stop your use and there's little you can do about it, while a written easement will show that you have legal right to use the land, it should also be part of your property deed when it's drawn up for the sale. You'll also want to have a clause in there that transfers the right to future heirs and owners, this will cover your property in case something happens to you and someone else inherits it or the easement will become invalid.

Do not assume that the easement will be given because it seems common sense. You'll also need an easement for pipes, cables and any hookups needed to utilities which may be required by law. There may also be easements on the land you're looking to buy already which affect where you want to build.

Water

If you're building in a suburban area then it's quite likely you'll simply need to hook into the local water and sewage system like any other construction. This is something most plumbers can advice you on and the utilities companies can mark the pipes and arrange for service. On the other hand, if you're in a rural area you may be considering well water and septic systems.

Florida recently had a case about a woman who had made her home self sufficient. The county ended up condemning the house because she refused to reconnect it to the local water company saying that her rainwater collection was adequate. While this seems extreme some locations require that you are connected whether you want well water or not and this may require the aforementioned easements for pipes. It also may be illegal to collect rainwater where you are. Some states have laws that mean the local government owns all water rights so you can't use the water on your land even though you own the land. This is something you can also discuss with your local planning office.

If you're going to put in a well/septic system then it's essential to do a dye test. What a dye test does is it lets you determine the drainage of the land. This is especially important if you're using a sewage system and water source on the same land as you don't want those two to get contaminated. A dye test is performed by digging a hole and pouring water dyed with special chemicals into it. If the water doesn't drain at a certain rate then the land doesn't drain well and your home is likely to get flooded in heavy weather. When the hole drains you'll be able to see where it comes out in the local water sources. This could be a creek a few feet away or in a lake a mile down the road. There's absolutely no telling where it will come out but your local authorities won't give you the permits for a septic system without one of these tests and will not be able to build on that land.

Resources

When buying land you would think you own everything in it, on it, and below it, but this is often not the case. Minerals, oil, timber and even the air on the land all has explicit rights which will be set out in your deed. Mineral rights probably isn't something you've thought about but should something valuable like oil be found there the state may then buy you out with compulsory purchase and force you to move. They don't even have to give you notice since it's in the deed, which means you could come home to your land already being ripped apart and a notice telling you that it's not yours anymore.

Similarly, timber and trees on your land aren't necessarily yours. If the previous owner negotiated a timber contract that included your land then this will stand even if you've purchased the property. It's important to know if there is an outstanding contract and how much timber they can take and from where. This can cause drainage challenges as trees help keep flooding from happening and deforestation may leave the land unsuited for building.

Pollution, Utilities, and Easements

While we've already looked at access easements there are also a few things to think about in regards to having your land connected to the public utilities and waste systems if the state or county requires it. Similarly, just because the land looks pristine it may have been previously used for chemical testing, spraying or other uses which means living on it could be hazardous to your health. While you may have some allowances for utilities (like the ability to drill a well) other things such as not having power lines nearby could be a challenge Wind turbines and solar are great alternatives for rural areas but there are often requirements or permits that need to be followed, and the local authority still may not allow you to have them since it will damage the view.

In the news right now there's a lot about pipelines and their impact on the land. The DAPL is a great example of this. The pipeline itself is not scheduled to go through Navajo land, yet the nation is protesting and so are many supporters. The reason they have a right to be upset is that even though the pipeline itself isn't on their land they are close enough that a spill from the pipeline could potentially contaminate their lands and destroy them, rendering the water useless and destroying industry and livestock. Their land is affected simply by proximity. The same is true of crop spraying and pesticides. Though your land itself may not be sprayed, by proximity you may be affected. Remember the story of Erin Brokovitch?

Legal Protection

When you buy an electronic from the store you're counting on two things – the store's return policy, and the manufacturers warranty. These two things make you feel safe buying the item because if anything goes wrong your money and the item are protected. Many people skip out on this step when buying land because they either don't know it exists or don't want to pay the extra cost. Start by looking at other pieces of land in the area and make sure the price of yours is in line with everything else, there's probably a reason if it's exceptionally cheap or expensive. You'll also want to insist on an Escrow for the funds until the transaction is complete as this will protect your money and help you get it back if there's a problem. Remember to actually look at the land too, as a topography map can only tell you so much and there may be rocks which can hamper construction and leveling.

Most people skip title insurance, but while there's always a backup for your paperwork at the public registry they may not have the complete document or any updates. There's also a lot of legal jargon here which is why it can be daunting. Title insurance and escrow together will mean that the money you pay only goes to the seller if the transaction works out – I.e the land is exactly what they say it is, and the title is as declared. It's essential when buying land because this is the document which tells you all of the information above and gives you the PID to work with the local authorities and utilities.

Chapter 3 – Your Containers

At the beginning of the book we looked at the different shapes and types of containers, and while it's pretty obvious that they're essentially large steel boxes. The standard sizes are 20, 40 and 45 foot containers and these come in either a standard height of High Cube which gives you an added foot in height, something that's almost essential if you're adding inside pipes and insulation as this will quickly eat up that space. Most manufacturers have a tolerance of +-5mm so these numbers are not exact.

External Dimensions

	Length	Width	Height
Standard 20 Foot	19'10 1/2" (6.06m)	8' (2.44m)	8'6" (2.59m)
Standard 40 Foot	40' (12.19m)	8' (2.44m)	8'6"(2.59m)
High Cube 20 Foot	19'10 1/2" (6.06m)	8' (2.44m)	9'6" (2.90m)
High Cube 40 Foot	40' (12.19m)	8' (2.44m)	9'6" (2.90m)

Internal Dimensions

	Length	Width	Height
Standard 20 Foot	19' 4 (5.89m)	7' 8 (2.34m)	7'10 (2.39m)
Standard 40 Foot	39' 5 (12.01m)	7' 8 (2.34m)	7'10 (2.39m)
High Cube 20 Foot	19' 4 (5.89m)	7' 8 (2.34m)	8'10 (2.69m)
High Cube 40 Foot	39' 5 (12.01m)	7' 8 (2.34m)	8'10 (2.69m)

While almost all types of containers are readily available in port areas you may not find such availability locally. Your budget may be the bottom line as to which you can afford rather than which you want.

The first decision you'll want to make is whether you want to buy new or "one trip", really they're almost the same. One trip containers have only been used once and generally don't get a lot of damage to them before being sold on. However, the fact that they have been used makes a big difference in price. This also means they will have a significantly longer lifespan than those that are marketed as used and will also lower the likelihood that your container has been treated with chemicals or pesticides.

Inspecting the Container

Never buy a container sight unseen, it's not safe and you do not know what you're getting. Make sure you inspect the exact container you plan on purchasing. You'll be able to tell this by the identification code. These are an 11 digit number marked into the container itself. The number has a very specific makeup and allows you to trace that containers journey and whether the company is telling the truth about it being new or one trip rather than used. The first three letters of the number tell you the owner of the container; the fourth letter determines the product itself and is usually a U, Z or J. U stands for shipping container while Z denotes a container trailer and J is equipment that is attached such as a refrigeration unit. After this there will be a six digit serial and a check digit at the end that marks a complete number. It should look like this:

Start your inspection looking for scars, scratches, dents, spots, and rust marks. Check any areas that look like they've been repainted. If the information is available find out what the previous cargo was. Also look for anything that looks like damage, while you may be able to get a discount for that it can also affect the lifespan and structure of your home. Try and purchase all your containers from the same manufacturer as this will help make sure dimensions are as uniform as possible.

Where to Purchase

The easiest way to purchase your container is through a dealer. These are plentiful in port areas but can be found all over the country. Green Cube Network is an easy search tool that specializes in shipping container recycling, but a simple Google search will give you other options. Reputable dealers are the best choice for most people because they have a certain guarantee to them that no other method has.

Online

There's plenty of easy online options to buy the containers however, it's unlikely you'll be able to see the container in person until it's delivered. While there are plenty of trustworthy sellers out there this is a risky choice as there's no real guarantee you're getting the exact same container pictured especially when it comes to overseas companies. Ebay, Gumtree, and Alibaba are just a couple of the most common sites you can search and purchase containers through.

Buying online gives you convenience but you've got to rely on reviews and reputation to find out if you're getting the real deal. Not to mention that until you stand inside a container those are just numbers for dimensions and it's a lot harder to get an idea of how much space you really have. Another challenge with buying online, and this is especially true with Alibaba, is that the containers may not be local, which means you'll incur the shipping charge of shipping the container to you which drives up the cost. It's hugely expensive which is exactly why many containers are "one trip" for example a container coming from China could cost you as much as $23,000 just to ship it to you in the US.

Direct

It's not a good idea to buy containers direct because they generally don't want to sell you one or two containers. If you do find a company willing to sell so little (remember most of these companies have thousands of containers at any given time) the price is likely to be higher than that of a dealer since the dealer gets a better offer for buying in bulk. Distributors and dealers only deal in containers which means they can get them from multiple sources, while many companies will not sell direct to the public.

You'll be able to find companies with a simple online search or just in the local yellow book. If you can't find anyone locally call a company that is not local and ask them if they know any dealers or distributors who might be local or willing to work locally. The local docks are also another alternative and they may also sell containers themselves.

Cost

In chapter 1 we looked at the rough cost of a shipping container. As of 2017 the rates are approximately as follows:

- Used Standard 20 Foot Container: US$2,100 | AUD$2,700 | GBP£1,350
- New Standard 20 Foot Container: US$3,000 | AUD$3,900 | GBP£1,950
- Used Standard 40 Foot Container: US$2,850 | AUD$3,650 | GBP£1,850
- New Standard 40 Foot Container: US$5,600 | AUD$7,200 | GBP£3,650
- Used High Cube 20 Foot Container: US$2,200 | AUD$2,850 | GBP£1,450
- New High Cube 20 Foot Container: US$3,200 | AUD$4,150 | GBP£2,100
- Used High Cube 40 Foot Container: US$2,950 | AUD$3,800 | GBP£1,925
- New High Cube 40 Foot Container: US$5,800 | AUD$7,500 | GBP£3,795

Once you've purchased your container you'll need to find a suitable delivery date.

Docks and distributors don't like these laying around so your delivery time may be as little as a few days so you'll need to be ready. The ground has to be prepared and everything has to be laid out so that it can be sat in place as soon as it arrives.

Chapter 4 – Preparing the Land

Before you can place your container you'll need to prepare some form of foundation. This will provide a stable, level surface for the container to sit on. While there are three suitable types of foundations not all local authorities will accept all three and you may have no choice but to use a certain type only. Ideally you'll want a qualified expert and engineer to lay your foundations as they will know how to deal with soil, codes and the land topography itself. The three main types used for container homes are pile, raft, and concrete pier foundations. This is another area where you don't want to compare the shipping container to a mobile home as they are usually much heavier which requires a different type of reinforcement in the concrete.

Foundations

The two most important considerations when laying foundation are cost and structure. Structurally you need to consult a professional as they will know best about distributing the weight of your container. With softer soil your foundation needs to be deeper as this adds more stability while hard soil or rock may only require leveling and minor foundation work. There's a tendency to over-spec foundations too which means making them stronger than is strictly necessary simply for peace of mind.

Concrete Piers

These are often similar to what is used for shed and small outbuildings, and they're often the cheapest type of foundation because they require the least materials. In the most basic these are concrete piers which contain reinforced steel bars that are placed strategically. The steel bars or occasionally steel mesh add to the stability and strength of the concrete. If you are planning on DIYing the foundation this is the easiest way to go because it requires the least concrete and least scientific approach. These piers should be placed anywhere that the "load" or main weight of the containers will be – the middle and the corners generally. If you're placing more than one container together you may want to place additional piers at the seams of the two so that both are fully supported. An average of 6 piers per container is standard.

Slab-on-Grade

Raft foundation is significantly more expensive but it's more stable than piers, the reason for this is that the entire container is supported on a concrete raft rather than perched. However, it also requires some digging into the top soil. The raft foundation is still quite quick to build and is a better idea where temperatures don't drop below freezing much as this lower ground temperature can affect the concrete. It also means that the concrete is prone to getting cold and allowing heat to leach away from your container which is why it's not ideal for cold climates since this will drive up your heating bill. The slab is less affected by bugs and termites as well since there's no wood involved. However, if you're planning on using a slab foundation you MUST have your utilities embedded into the slab and the connections placed exactly to connect with those inside the container since there will be no access to them once the concrete has set and no way to lay them afterward.

Pile Foundation

Similar to concrete piers these are deeper and more structurally challenging which is why they tend to be the most expensive. This is the type of foundation necessary when your soil is weak and not suitable for a solid slab. There's a great design study with a container home using these called the Graceville Container Home Study which centered around a family whose original home was devastated in flooding and they needed a cheaper rebuilding alternative. Their home was a three layer 6000ft design that featured everything from a pool and gym to a studio. They needed the deeper piles because of the flood and cyclone risk.

The piles are solid cylindrical steel tubes which are hammered down until they are in more solid ground. One they are secured they are filled with concrete and steel rebar which resembles the same as the piers above ground. This is not a construction that can be done DIY because of the need for a pile driver. Since this is the most secure it is recommended to use this type of foundation anyway if you are doing a multiple stacked design as it will provide extra support.

Strip Foundation

Less common is a combination of slab and pier known as strip foundations. These are strips of thick concrete laid out either on part of the container footprint or around the whole thing. This is a cheaper alternative than a slab but more stable than piers. This is a good choice when the ground is wetter as the inside area being open allows for better drainage. They are however, less stable than a pile foundation and prone to slippage in high winds or earthquakes since the container can slide. They're quite shallow as well which means they're not suited for stacked container designs.

Concrete

Concrete comes in many grades, and if you've ever looked at the hardware store you'll see many different types. When it comes to building a foundation you'll need to use a specific strength of concrete based on your land. The strength is measured in C with a number after it; the higher the number the stronger the concrete. C15 is general purpose concrete while C30 is a much stronger concrete. C15 uses 1 part cement to 2 parts of sand and 5 gravel, the amount of cement used increases the strength of the concrete. It's easy to mix small amounts by hand but for piers and slabs you will need a concrete mixer or to order ready-mix delivered. This does increase the cost of your concrete but it insures that you don't have one chunk of concrete already dried while you're still mixing it. You must mix it properly together so that it is thoroughly combined or you risk having different structural densities which can cause cracks and weaken over time.

Calculating the amount of concrete needed is fairly simple, you need to know how many square feet your concrete area covers and then mix accordingly. For a 20' container, for example, if you were placing it on a raft foundation that was 2 feet deep and just wider than the container you would want an area that was 10'x22'x2' or 440 cubed feet of concrete. When the concrete is mixed it begins a curing process that eventually hardens and sets it. This typically takes between 5-

7 days and requires some moisture to be added to prevent it from drying out too quickly on top and cracking. During the curing period the weather and temperature needs to remain fairly constant and both extreme hot and cold can affect the curing process.

In hot weather you'll need some form of shade to protect it from direct sunlight and the ground should be sprayed with cold water before pouring. The concrete itself should be mixed with cold water and if possible laid in the evening or early morning to avoid the heat of the day.

In cold weather (below 0C for three consecutive days), make sure any frost or standing water is cleared from the foundation area first. Then lay the concrete and cover with an insulating blanket layer immediately. The blankets should remain on for the entire curing time before being removed gradually to raise the temperature slowly and prevent cracking.

Footings

Soil Bearing Capacities	
Class of Materials	Load-Bearing Pressure (pounds per square foot)
Crystalline bedrock	12,000
Sedimentary rock	6,000
Sandy gravel or gravel	5,000
Sand, silty sand, clayey sand, silty gravel, and clayey gravel	3,000
Clay, sandy clay, silty clay, and clayey silt	2,000
Source: Table 401.4.1; CABO One- and Two- Family Dwelling Code; 1995.	

Within the concrete you will need footings. These are there to support the foundation and prevent it from settling unevenly and cracking. These are essentially the "feet" that your foundation rests on and are usually 16-20" wide. These are better in good load bearing soil but if your soil has an uneven distribution you may have to place different footings across your foundation to make sure it stays solid. When the footing isn't centered properly or the ground is uneven the weight of the building above pushes down and will eventually cause the footing to give way, making the foundation crack. This is almost always determined by an engineer, and even they sometimes get it wrong. The footings are tied very strongly to the type of soil and its bearing capacity.

Footings should be placed a minimum of 6" below where the frost line in the ground is. When the earth freezes it shifts slightly which means that a footing placed above this line will move with temperature changes. This is especially important if you're planning a shallow foundation. You can find the information for your geographic frost line at the National Snow and Ice Data Center which shows the ground parameters and soil classifications. The average footing comes in one of three sizes (plus frost line depth):

- 8" x 16" x 16"
- 12" x 24" x 24"
- 10" x 20" x 20"

Each footing is constructed separately usually starting with those which are higher if the design is leveling a slope. The footings are made using 1/2" rebar which is 8" longer than the depth of the concrete. Once the footing hole is dug the rebar is driven or hammered into the ground so that the top of the rebar is level with the intended top of the concrete. The rebar should be placed every few inches and the amount of rebar will depend on how big your footings are.

Minimum Width of Concrete or Masonry Footings (inches)						
	Load-Bearing Value of Soil (psf)					
	1,500	2,000	2,500	3,000	3,500	4,000
Conventional Wood Frame Construction						
1-story	16	12	10	8	7	6
2-story	19	15	12	10	8	7
3-story	22	17	14	11	10	9
4-Inch Brick Veneer Over Wood Frame or 8-Inch Hollow Concrete Masonry						
1-story	19	15	12	10	8	7
2-story	25	19	15	13	11	10
3-story	31	23	19	16	13	12
8-Inch Solid or Fully Grouted Masonry						
1-story	22	17	13	11	10	9
2-story	31	23	19	16	13	12
3-story	40	30	24	20	17	15
Source: Table 403.1: CABO One- and Two- Family Dwelling Code; 1995.						

While this table is intended on applying to standard construction the load bearing values compared to the heaviest construction will give you an idea for the expected bearing of each footing. Sometimes your footings aren't perfect and if it is off center in good soil it may not be a problem, however if the footing isn't centered correctly for the foundation it will need to be fixed either using gravel, an additional steel tie or re-augmenting the footing.

If you find you have a soft spot, one where the rebar simply disappears, you may need to excavate and create a pile for that specific footing rather than a pier construction. An alternative is to excavate the soft soil completely and fill the hole back in with gravel or a lower grade concrete. You cannot simply increase the width of the footing without changing the thickness which can cause the concrete to crack.

In fact, there's so much potential that needs to be correct about footings on it's own that it could fill a book.

Fixing the Container

Whichever foundation you have chosen you'll need a solid way of attaching the container. The best way of doing this is by attaching a steel plate into the concrete before it is cured. The steel plate should have vertical bars that sink into the concrete and will add stability. After the curing process has finished the container can be welded directly onto these steel plates. The plates should be a minimum of 1/4" to 1/2" thick, with thicker plates being stronger. You will still see the top of the plate and this needs to be level across the entire foundation. There are some local codes that apply to this when it comes to metal plates and grades for attachment screws so it's good to do some research if you're DIYing.

An alternative to welding plates is simply to bolt the container directly into the concrete with anchors. This is much simpler and cheaper, however, it is not as strong. You can also use J hooks to attach the container to the exposed rebar in the concrete directly. Concrete anchors are the weakest choice but they can also be an added safety measure if you do these and plate welding.

There is no hard rule about fixing the container to the foundation, and if you're planning on potentially moving the container at a later date you may choose not to. There is nothing wrong with simply placing the container on top of the foundation but there is a distinct lack of stability and this may affect your home insurance at a later date if it's found to be a factor with damage. Welding makes the containers much harder to remove if you want your home to be portable.

Chapter 5 – Crafting the Container

If you're creating a simple one container home then you're ready to look into insulation and more, otherwise you'll need to know about fitting more than one container together. Not only that but how can you make this steel box into a livable home? It takes more than just throwing a couch in to make this pass inspection as a viable place to live. Even if your container is only temporary you need it to be properly insulated and crafted or you're going to get some very nasty action from the local authorities.

Connecting Containers

When choosing your containers you should have selected those from the same manufacturer with similar dimensions in height, while you can connect containers from other manufacturers there's a greater chance of error which means getting creative if they're just too different. If you've submitted a plan to the local building department this is the stage at which you have to follow it clearly or you may find that they require you to stop building work and reapply. You can either buy container joining kits or do it yourself. When it comes to joining containers you need to understand the construction of them. A container is a unibody design which means it's made up of about 15 separate elements that all work together to make a single container. It's extremely efficient from an engineering view.

Stacking, Clustering or Both

Depending on your design you may want to put your containers on top of each other. Shipping containers are rated to stack up to 10 high without additional reinforcement or adjustment. However, the moment you remove doors or start adjusting the shape and any elements of the container from an engineering standpoint it's no longer the same thing and once it's been modified the strength changes. Some things just aren't possible. A single container on it's own is quite limited when it comes to design and may not be practical for the average family. Grouping multiple containers into a modular design is the easiest way to enlarge the space.

Look at the normal use for containers – they're frequently stacked and able to withstand hurricane force wind in their intended design. Looking at standard containers in use will give you the golden rules of stacking – the design has to be even, and the load distributed properly. Most containers are stacked directly on top of each other. It's boxy, but it's very strong and functional. Containers are only ever stacked like to like in their normal use, never with an unmodified container on the bottom crosswise and never with a smaller container on the bottom. A smaller container is also never stacked on top of a larger container. The reason for this is that the corrugated steel on top of the container is only rated for basic maintenance or the weight of a human walking across the top not another container or a max of 200kg. When containers are stacked their weight is distributed through the internal and external load bearing beams which line up directly with each container like for like. If this alignment doesn't happen then the load is not distributed evenly and it can cause the weight to buckle.

If you place a container in any way other than this the force does not distribute properly, and if you're not convinced just look at videos of overloading containers. You'll see the bottom one is often squashed almost flat. So imagine if that was your home with you in it!

Never stack unmodified containers without adding support!

You've probably seen designs that go against this golden rule – containers that have the upper forward of the lower, the upper container at an angle or even criss cross across the top. The simple fact is that all irregular stacking needs modifications to distribute the weight. It's quite complex which requires a structural engineer. Since most designs are unique it is something that can only be configured by engineers and architect.

Photograph by plentyofants
(https://www.flickr.com/photos/plentyofants/683994728)

Looking at the above design you can see that these containers do not follow the rule. On the bottom layer you can also see additional yellow painted I beams that are part of the structural reinforcement and again on the far left to help hold the third level up. These 22 containers are not standing on their weight alone and there's likely significant reinforcement inside as well. Reinforcement is required on all the containers. If you want an edgy look like this it is going to be costly, even if it's just two containers.

From a practical standpoint, stacking two containers directly on top of each other is the cheapest and most secure design. Side by side is also equally effective compared to trying to connect any other way.

When placing containers side by side there's often a challenge getting both containers to fit flush. The ISO corner fittings protrude out which causes a gap between the containers because the design puts the weight on these corners. The gap obviously is a problem and it's quite clumsy to fill it. The best way to deal with it is to simply weld inverted angle steel between the roofs and flat bar on the sides and floor. The reason for this is that you don't want to let water get into the join between the two containers since the container roof is slightly angled. This means that when the containers are stacked you create a trap for water to get stuck in which will eventually cause corrosion and structural damage.

An alternative for joining containers side by side is something called Backer Rod, a soft material that can be pushed into the jam like Play Doh and the covered up. The Backer Rod goes directly into the gap between the two containers.

Not all containers are exactly square, this is especially true of older containers as they may have warped or been damaged which will change the shape just enough that they can't be stacked easily. This is especially true of the floors as two container floors may not line up evenly.

Interior Considerations

When modifying a container structure it needs to be sturdy enough and secure enough that when it's lifted onto the slab it doesn't disintegrate. The biggest force the home will ever face is when it is lifted and moved which is why many choose to modify the containers after they have been set in place. If you're planning on stacking containers this may not be possible though. Most modifications for stacked containers require an engineer, and take more than common sense but clustered side-by side modification is pretty easy to DIY.

Side Wall Modification

The sidewall panels are not intended on being modified, and this affects the loading capacity of the structure. There's not a lot of tests on this because of the amount of flexibility with design here.

Modification should be done with caution. The metal panels of the side wall are made up of 11 different pieces and these will expand and contract with weather. By removing part of the panel you're changing the forces affecting the wall and sometimes you'll need to have additional reinforcement just while cutting to stop the container roof sagging and this can create memory. The side walls are made of 1.6mm corrugated steel and it's heavy so be careful moving it as it can act like a guillotine.

You can remove up to 8-10ft at most from each side wall safely without adding extra reinforcement for the roof, but it's still advised for longevity. Removing more than 10 feet needs structural support or your roof will begin to sag. This is especially important if you're planning on stacking because it creates a huge weak spot which will cave under the weight of another container. It's a good idea for doors to leave about 8" from the ceiling to the top of the door to help with structural support even if you're adding additional beams. This is particularly important if your containers don't have side beams and even then you may need reinforcement for the roof. Check the outside of your container – there will either be a thick steel bar on the outside or not. If there is then you have a little better support than if you do not. Companies have been cutting down on using this bar as it creates the same shape with slightly less steel and is cheaper to produce.

After the internal wall has been cut it will need to be ground to even the edges and then welded to the other container. The edges need to be cleaned up so that they are as even as possible and a simple steel disc cutter is fine for this. You'll need about a 2″ wide strip to seal the container gap at the floor level. This isn't structural and you should expect a slight lip to the join but once you add your intended flooring surface this should be hidden. Expanding foam is ideal for filling in the gap at the sides internally – externally it should already be welded like the roof or joined using Backer Rod. You may want to clamp the walls together while this is curing to keep the wall in place.

Windows and Doors

Cutting window holes is much like side wall modification, you're affecting the structural integrity and may need reinforcement. The easiest way to do this is to stiffen the metal around the window or door hole which will prevent warping or bending. You'll also need to add a method of attaching standard window and door frames. The easiest way to do this is to create a steel box frame and then weld this into the cut out of the container. This gives you both reinforcement and something to work into which is comparable to wooden designs.

Windows often have poor insulation values and this also needs to be taken into account. Adding windows and doors is much like the internal modification – you'll need to grind the cut down, reinforce it as necessary, and then weld a frame into place if needed. You can also check out a company called Cube Depot which specializes in modifications for container homes. Standard windows are just basic frames which would normally slot into wooden framing and be screwed in. You can still do this, but you'll need to attach them to a metal frame and seal the gap so no moisture can get in. This also means a slight lip to prevent drips getting between the frame and the window itself.

The placement of your windows can also be strategic as the right placement allows for cross ventilation in good weather but won't cause too much heat to be lost in winter. These should be done in the planning stage and already laid out before construction starts. Consider the desired internal layout as well since this may affect where you want the windows. Building codes may also apply to the number and size of the windows so check this during the planning stage as well. Some authorities require a number of windows or a certain amount of light to be let into the home and you'll need to talk with the building planning authority when designing your home to make sure you're complying with this or you may end up having to redesign.

You can also consider adding skylights if you're not stacking your containers. These will still affect structural integrity and should be light and able to drain water away from the roof so you don't end up with standing water or moss that damages the steel over time. These are a great way of adding natural light to areas inside your container which may not be suitable for windows. Not all skylights are suitable for containers and this is a case-by-case on the design – just remember you don't want water to pool and you'll need them airtight enough to prevent heat loss or condensation.

Obviously you'll want some form of door to your home and most people choose not to use the latch doors that come with the container but to use the steel elsewhere. This leaves a large open space which will need to be filled. There are several options but most people choose traditional doors and framing or rolling doors. You'll also want to consider security with a lockbox or with a welded area into the frame so the door can't simply be kicked in.

Rollup

Rollup doors are similar to electric garage doors and can be between 4-10ft wide. They have sliding clasp locks and are made of 26" galvanized steel or aluminum. They're a much more industrial looking choice.

The first thing is to set the rails. You'll want to measure the door with an added inch between the rails. You should attach the rails by snapping lines into the container wall at the correct height for the rails to be fitted into. Then grind the surface so that the wall has a good surface to attach the rail to. Mark the container at the top where the bolt holes are on the rail so you know where to weld to and grind the paint off to have a clean welding surface. Clamp the rails into place on the wall and tack weld them into place before removing the clamps. Check the door and make sure there are markings that clearly state left and right so that you hang the door on the right way. Attach the door to the top of the wall above the rails with bolts but do not tighten them down until you're sure it's in the correct place. Push the door flush against the container as you tighten then bend the tabs over so that the door drops in easier. Unhook the door and remove the banding before dropping it into the tracks and unwinding the door. Check the tracks by looking in the sight holes on the rails, you should see the door in the center of the hole all the way down, if you need to fix any holes break the nearest tack on the rail and adjust the edge so that the door will align to the door. Roll the door back up before welding the rails properly including welding where the bolts for the door are as additional support.

The door is now attached, but you'll need to adjust the spring tension and add hardware. The spring tension is adjusted by a large nut on the end of the bar where the door rolls up. Turn the nut so that the door opens and closes a little before attaching the stop brackets. The door should be tensioned so that at the halfway point it rolls itself up and it rolls itself down with only a little help. It should feel like it's trying to pull itself up when it's not latched down.

Most rollup doors come with instructions for installation so you should follow those, especially for additional hardware.

The biggest challenge you face with a rollup door is insulation, as most traditional methods will not work and won't be very nice to look at either.

Traditional Door

Traditional residential doors are usually made of wood, and while you can get all steel doors they're often much more expensive. The typical dimensions are 3 feet wide by about 7 feet in height. These can be attached much like windows with a steel frame being welded into the container wall cut out and then bolted in as would normally be done with wood. This is by far the most aesthetic option and it also allows for better insulation since you're not cutting a large chunk from the wall. It will also allow you to put windows next to the door in the open end space.

Chapter 6 – Insulation

Containers have to be insulated. It's not an option to skip this but how your container is insulated will vary based on where you plan on living. Insulation is usually found with two ratings – R and U. The R value is the resistance of the material to changes in temperature, meaning higher R numbers are more effective insulators. U value measures the opposite, it is the amount of heat lost through various methods. The higher the U value the less insulating the material is and the less effective. The most common materials for insulation are panels, blanket batts or fiberglass in building construction but container homes also allow for expanding or spray foam insulation inside. The container itself has an R value of 0.33 while fiberglass has a rating of 3.14, so you can see why the container needs to be insulated.

There's a lot of choice in materials but you'll want to consult the local building codes for sure to make sure you're using the right materials.

Framing the container

You need something to attach your insulation to inside the container which is why you need framing. This same method is used inside standard construction and creates a series of pockets where insulation is attached and eventually paneling over it. This is especially important if you're in a cold climate. Start the process by welding any holes closed. It's actually quite easy but you need to be precise. Using 2x4's create 2 feet wide spaces from the floor to ceiling, and surround any windows or doors with the same framing. Screw the frame directly into the container At this stage you should be adding wiring, pipes etc before putting in the insulation. Your frame adds several inches into the container itself and this is the ideal space to fit pipes and wires.

Once the framing is in place fill the space with your chosen insulation and add panels on top, remembering to cut out holes for electronic fixtures and water pipes as needed.

Fiberglass

Fiberglass insulation comes in rolls that are 2 feet wide and cost approximately

$40. They have ratings from R10-R30 and you can choose anything on that scale based on how well insulated you want it to be. These also come in pallet loads so determine the exact area you want to cover before buying as this might be cheaper. It's made up of a glass composite that is very light and foamy. Glass is spun into small fibers that are then woven into mats and comes in a variety of colors. These come in rolls or batts. Batts are large chunks of insulation that is already shaped to fit into 2ft framing and it has a foil backing that faces the warmth to help reflect it back and prevent heat escaping. This creates a membrane which prevents moisture and stops small fiberglass particles getting into the living area. Thicker batts offer better resistance but they will also shrink the space inside the container so you'll have to compromise.

It is a hazardous building material as small particle exposure can cause breathing issues and skin irritation. Symptoms include rashes, itchiness, nose bleeds, respiratory problems and it has also been linked to cancer and serious infections. OSHA has a warning label on fiberglass and you should always wear protective breathing and eye protection before touching it or installing it. A humidifier which dampens the air can also prevent particles from getting airborne. You'll also want to wash your hands and skin down with cold water afterward as warm water will open pores up which can force particles further into the skin.

Foam

Spray foam outperforms fiberglass in all insulation tests and comes in two main types – closed and open cell foam. It creates an air and insulation barrier just like fiberglass batts and is effective as long as it's installed properly. Spray foam has to be a certain thickness to be effective which is why it's not ideal for conditions where you need extra insulation. You also need to make sure that there is no air leakage between the foam and the container and that if the foam contracts in cold weather it isn't pulling away from the frame.

Closed cell foams have a higher R value but they're harder to see if the entire cavity has been filled and you'll need to spot check it to make sure it's covering the entire framing space. Open foam expands to fill the cavity which makes it easier to use. With closed cell the coverage has to be uniform thickness or heat will travel through the less insulated areas. Lat or lumpy insulation is a good sign that this isn't even. It's imperative if you use spray insulation that they do not miss any areas as the colder steel will attract humidity and condensation which can then lead to rust over time. A great way to check there are no leaks in your insulation is to do a fog test with a simple fog machine. If you seal the container and see fog escaping from anywhere then you know the insulation is not fully sealed since it's supposed to be air tight.

A spray foam installer should know the envelope of the building (edges and shape) so that they can spray properly in conditioned and non conditioned areas without simply spraying the entire interior needlessly. It's one of the most expensive types of insulation so you don't want to add it if you don't need it. You can also spray insulation on the outside and underneath of your building too if you plan on making it look like traditional construction and covering it as this will add an extra layer outside.

There are several different types of foam insulation but cellulose is the most eco-friendly. It's made from straw, sawdust, cotton, hemp, recycled newspapers and other materials which have been treated to make them flame retardant. It's much less expensive than fiberglass and there's very few health risks associated with it. While there is come gassing off it's not as bad a concern as the glass particles but you'll still want breathing and protective equipment.

Panel Insulation

This is the easiest type of insulation and it fits easily into framing. These are presized panels that you slot in to the gaps in the frame much like blanket or fiberglass. They're more expensive though because they're thinner but provide much the same R ratings. The normal R rating for panel insulation is 7.5 so it outperforms fiberglass and has a thinner depth which won't eat into your storage container. It's cheaper than spray insulation but still more expensive.

Blanket Insulation

This is the cheapest form of insulation and is essentially rolls of thick shredded fabric or rock wool. The insulation is pushed in ready formed batts into the gaps in the frame. The challenge is that it is very thick and will eat into your wall space. Some blanket insulation is made of fiberglass and requires safety measures. Wool and cotton are some of the most eco-friendly choices if you don't want to pay for cellulose foam. These natural choices will still make the R rating needed for construction standards and generally cost the same while being more eco-friendly.

Living Roof

While there's not going to be a section on roofing because it's such an optional design choice, adding a living roof can significantly improve the insulation of your container. A living roof is one made out of plants and moss which creates a barrier between the outside elements and the container itself. This is great for keeping the temperature of the container down in hot climates but doesn't help with insulation in colder climbs as the roof may actually cause heat to escape faster.

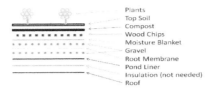

Plants
Top Soil
Compost
Wood Chips
Moisture Blanket
Gravel
Root Membrane
Pond Liner
Insulation (not needed)
Roof

Living roofs can be flat or sloped but a sloped design is better for shipping containers as it encourages water run off so no standing water damages the steel. Living roofs can add up to 150kg/m² so this is not advised if you've made significant structural changes to your container without reinforcement as it could cause the roof to buckle.

This is the basic layout of a living roof. The insulation is recommended for a shipping container because there's more chance of heat and cool escaping, and in this case foam insulation really is best externally because it creates a water-tight barrier. Plants need moisture but this is exactly what you don't need for your steel container. The pond liner is an added barrier to help stop that moisture getting down to container level. There's a great Instructable about building a living roof which explains the entire process and different levels.

Conclusion

Steel container design is innovative and often eco friendly, but there's no reason why you have to be limited by the basic steel box. Unlike traditional modular construction there's a lot of engineering concerns when using containers which is why most people prefer companies or pre-fab to do the deal for them. Shipping container homes add a fun element and a more secure element to what would otherwise just be another house.

Before buying anything, make sure your local authorities will allow you to build with such an alternative material. The best thing you can do is plenty of research and bring examples and diagrams with you when speaking to the authorities.

The most important part about a shipping container home is the structure, it's the reason you chose the home after all! Using steel has both benefits and pitfalls and it's important to weigh those with your requirements and budget before settling on a shipping container construction.

Remember, that these are industrial containers and they may have been exposed to noxious materials so make sure that all hazardous chemicals are gone before you move in. Buying new containers isn't in the spirit of the movement but it can be a safer choice.

Hopefully, you've learned a lot about the construction processes that go into a shipping container home and are better armed to get started.

Preview of Shipping Container Homes: How to Move into a Shipping Container Home (a Step By Step Guide)

Introduction

Did you know that there are over 50 million surplus containers in the U.S? Yes, that's correct, and what that means for you is that there are more than enough containers available for you to build a home. Not only that, you'll be able to build a home for a lower price than if you were to go with a traditional home.

Let me guess, are you interested in moving into a shipping container because of the low cost of building this type of home? If so, great; because that's a significant benefit of building with shipping containers. Or perhaps you were attracted to shipping container homes because they are Eco-friendly? As you probably already know, they are excellent homes for the environment. Or perhaps you were attracted to the looks of shipping container homes? A lot of people think that they are the coolest building type out there.

People may also decide to move into a shipping container because of the speed of which you can build the home, compared to a brick and mortar home. Off the grid living is also something that attracts people to shipping container homes.

Whatever your motivation is, I'm here to help you to move into your shipping container home. I've produced this book in a step by step way so you can get clarity about all the processes.

We will go over two important chapters at the beginning of this book before we get into the step by step guide. I want to thank you for opening this book, and I'm confident that you'll receive a lot of value from it. Let's begin.

Chapter 1

Advantages and Disadvantages of Moving Into A Shipping Container Home

I'm not here to lecture you on whether or not you should move into a shipping container home. What I am here to do, however, is to provide all the information you need on how to move into a shipping container home. Therefore, it's important that you know the advantages as well as the disadvantages so you can be prepared. This will save you money, time and effort.

Advantages

- Shipping container homes are strong which means that they can endure harsh environments.

- Shipping containers are pretty easy to access, and they don't cost that much to buy.
- They are eco-friendly. Shipping containers can easily be recycled to save steel. You also don't need as much of the traditional building materials such as cement and bricks.
- Moving into a shipping container home can save you a lot of money compared to if you were to move into a regular home. You won't need as much labor since there is no such thing as attachments that needs to be drilled to the outer skin of the home.
- You can move your home. It's not easy to move a traditional home, is it? Now, it doesn't mean that it's always easy to move a shipping container homes since you might have footings, etc. But at least it's possible.

Disadvantages

- It can get really warm in a shipping container since it conducts heat much better than wood, brick or block structures. Insulation is, therefore, important which we will discuss later in the book.

- Rust can form unless the steel is well insulated and sealed.
- You'll most likely need building permits.
- The roof of the shipping container is not as strong. We've stated that one of the advantages is the strength of the container. However, it's important to note that its roof shouldn't hold more than 300 kg.
- The majority of shipping containers have wooden floors. These floors are often treated with hazardous chemicals (if the container is used). For example, pesticides to get pests away. The paint can also contain phosphorus or other harmful chemicals.

Alright, so you might get a little bit scared if you haven't heard about the last bullet point before. However, there are ways around this. For example, if you buy a new shipping container – simply tell your manufacturer to avoid hazardous chemicals. If you are buying a used shipping container, you can also cover the floor with non-breathable flooring underlayment. You can even remove the wooden floor if you want to be 100% safe. Regarding the paint issue, simply remove it! We will talk about insulation in chapter 11, but I will say right now that I recommend foam insulation since it can protect you from harmful chemicals.

A Shipping Container Building In A Nutshell

A shipping container provides a unit that it can be designed from. It's a given unit since your parameters are already set in terms of dimensions. But there is flexibility in how you arrange a shipping container. It provides instant space that is easy to install. Within a couple of days, you can have up to 10 shipping containers delivered to your site. You can have lockable space. And if you're an owner/builder, your time might be limited so you can always have a dedicated shipping container for storage of tools. And last but not least, they are available. It costs too much to recycle them all so your doing a great deed by moving into a shipping container home.

Chapter 2

6 Crucial Mistakes to Avoid When Moving into a Shipping Container Home

Before we go into more of the step by step of how to actually move into a shipping container home, I want to cover some common mistakes to avoid. By avoiding these mistakes, you can save thousands of dollars as well as valuable time. The following is mistakes that other people have done. As the saying goes, *it's better to learn from other people's mistakes than from your own.*

1. They do not look up local planning regulations. I heard a story once of a person that invested over $50 000 in getting a spectacular shipping container home. Not only that, he had spent two years on this project. Now, here's the problem. Once it was built, he got told that the house didn't comply with the local planning regulations. Perhaps this is an extreme example, but he just didn't know better. Now you know better. Always make sure to check with your local public works building division before you begin your project. However, before you meet with them, you need to have a good idea of the home that you want to build. You must also have an idea of a plot of land where you want to place your shipping container home. You have to check out the rules and standards where you live since they differentiate from country to country and state to state. In some states in the U.S, you don't even need a permit since they fall outside of city zoning. However, that's not the norm, so do your research.

2. People buy a container with the wrong height. I can't tell you how many times I've seen people make this mistake. So for example, they often go with regular height containers that are 8 foot and 6 inches tall. However, they often realize later on that there are actually containers that are 9 foot and 6 inches in height. Now, why should you go with the second option? The reason is that you don't have to sacrifice valuable head room when you are insulating the ceiling of the container. So go for a container with an extra foot in height, and you'll get 8-foot ceiling instead of 7-foot ceiling when you insulate.

3. They buy a container without actually seeing it first. This is a huge mistake that you definitely want to avoid. I know people that have bought containers over the phone or online without actually seeing them first. Most of them got lucky, but one of them got an old and beat up container that cost him a lot of money to repair. So for god sake, learn from his mistake and make sure that you always inspect the container that you're going to buy. Make sure that your container is as new as possible, hasn't been used for transporting chemicals and is waterproof.

4. They use the wrong type of insulation. The insulation that you should pick depends on the climate. For example, if you live where it rains a lot, you might want to have a seamless vapour barrier for spray foam as a part of your insulation. However, you might not want a vapour barrier if you live in a climate where it's really warm since you want your insulation to keep your container cool. Of course, the insulation also depends on your budget and what style you want, so pick it carefully. I've seen too many examples of people who have picked the wrong type of insulation. This has resulted in their home rusting and needing costly repairs. In some cases, they have also had it very cold during the winter or too hot during the summer.

5. They cut too much steel from the container. It might seem to be a smart idea to cut out a lot of steel to get a more spacious home. However, cutting too much out can be a costly mistake. It will cost you a lot of money to reinforce with steel beams if your container is too weak. Now, this doesn't mean that you need to worry about some windows and doors. It's okay to cut out steel for those things. But the problem arises when you start to cut out too much from the walls. If you're going to cut out a lot of steel, make sure you use support beams.

6. Choosing a contractor that doesn't do a great job. This mistake pretty much speaks for itself. But it's important that you choose your contractor with care. Also, make sure that you have basic knowledge about shipping container homes so you can have a good conversation with your contractor about your needs. This book is here to help you with that.

Now I know that you might already be aware of some of these mistakes. You may already have done research on your own. But these are worth repeating and as I said – I've seen too many people making these mistakes, and I wish better for you.

Chapter 3

Step 1: Hire or Build it Yourself?

The first step to building a shipping container home is to decide how you want to build it. Do you need help from a general contractor or can you do it yourself? Perhaps you've already decided how you want to do. But I still wanted to give you some information regarding this since it's the first step in the process of building a shipping container home. I will share some tips that can be useful if you decide to hire a general contractor – as well as some things to think about if you were to do it yourself.

Hiring a general contractor

This can be a great choice if you feel that you want someone with more experience to help you. Now, of course, it's going to cost you more than if you were to build it perfectly yourself. You do, however, have to factor in time. Because let's face it, your time is also worth money.

If you decide to go with a general contractor, please make sure that you talk to a lot of them. As I've stated in chapter 2, one of the biggest mistakes that people make when building a shipping container home is that they hire the wrong guy. You don't want to be part of that statistic. Instead, make calls and reach out to several different firms.

Now, there are three project delivery methods, here they are:

1. Design/Bid/Build
2. Construction Management, and Design/Build
3. Design and build

It's hard for me to say which one of these is best since it depends. But what I can say is that which one you chose might affect whether or not you get a fixed price or not. So that's something to ask you contractor about. The amount of design information and drawings prior to the build can also vary depending on the method used.

Make sure to hire someone who is licensed. If you do not do this, you run a risk of the project being classified as illegal and the project might be torn down because it doesn't fit with the required building regulations.

Build It Yourself
Generally speaking, this is most likely going to be your choice if you have a low budget, high craftsmanship and a lot of time to devote to this project.

Regardless of which method you choose, this book will help you, step by step. But it is, however, the first decision that you have to make. Can you build it? And do you want to build it? Or would you rather have someone else do it for you?

Check out this book!

Preview of Shipping Container Homes: A Comprehensive Guide To Shipping Container Homes

Introduction

Photograph   by   Aaron   Muszalski
(https://www.flickr.com/photos/sfslim/7427073926)

In 1956 the metal shipping container was born from the mind of Malcolm McLean, and while they were used for multiple purposes like storage, it wasn't until the 1980's that they were considered as a habitable building alternative. In the last few years, the concept has exploded.

Shipping container houses are contemporary, aesthetically different and fit the popular fad concept of "tiny homes." They are an alternative to traditional home construction and can save you money and time. But are they really viable?

Homes constructed from shipping containers are a trend that has exploded in recent years and only continues to grow in popularity. This book contains everything you need to know to turn your dream of living in a home constructed from shipping containers into a reality and whether or not it's really a worthwhile choice.

In this book, you will learn all the ins and outs of home construction using shipping containers. You'll learn all the advantages and disadvantages construction using this alternative material and why it is so popular all over the world. Find out how to buy a shipping container suitable for home construction and what you need to know before you purchase one. In this book, Shipping Container Homes: A Comprehensive Guide to Shipping Container Homes, you will discover advice and tips that will help you every step of the way. With this book, you will be ready to tackle any challenge and will ready to turn your dream of living in a shipping container home a reality.

Not only that but we'll look at whether their use as humanitarian homes is really worthwhile and whether the pros outweigh the cons. We've even covered a little about how container use has evolved over time to become the modern habitation choice many want today.

A shipping container home is something that pushes the boundaries of modern construction, and it's so out of the ordinary that the world is still buzzing about it even though it's been thirty years. Regardless of what piqued your interest in using shipping containers for home construction, you will find advice, solutions and important information contained in this book. You will learn the steps you will need to take to turn a shipping container into the home of your dreams. This books will guide through the process and help you to attain your goal of living in your own shipping container home.

Chapter 1 - Houses made from shipping containers

There is a movement in home design and construction that is going on worldwide. It began in the eighties and has gripped the imagination of all that have witnessed it. It is green, eco-conscious, and affordable. It has even been called chic, hip, contemporary survivalist, and in some cases, a little eccentric. It is bold, uncharted territory that is growing in popularity daily and gains followers and critics. What is this movement? In the simplest terms, it is the Tiny House Movement, but with a decided twist.

Tiny House

Photograph by Tammy Strobel
(https://www.flickr.com/photos/rowdykittens/8367839709)

The Tiny House Movement is a redefining of what it means to construct and own a home. Instead of purchasing large homes and spending well over six figures to live in huge residences with rooms full of clutter, many people have found an alternative - Tiny Houses. Tiny Houses are more affordable, sometimes movable and are approximately 500 square feet or less. They are built and maintained for much less than a traditional residence and are the dwelling of choice for people that choose to live simply, live well within their financial means, and live in harmony with nature.

Springing from the Tiny House Movement, it did not take long before shipping containers began to be used as the building blocks of residential structures. In the late eighties, the plans for the first shipping container home were drawn up, and history was made. Since that time, shipping container homes have branched off into many different areas and have split into a movement of their own.

Some container homes still retain their tiny house origins. Shipping containers fit into the tiny house specifications, can be built in remote locations, do not contain a lot of space, are built from a repurposed container and can be moved. Other container homes and structures have morphed into something very new, and exciting. They have been used for surf shacks, lakeside getaways, small houses, large homes, swimming pools, hotels, apartment buildings, libraries and art galleries, offices, Antarctic bases, underground bunkers, and the list goes on. In many countries, they are even being used to solve housing challenges such as for the construction of orphanages or to provide housing for the homeless or people that are the victims of natural disasters.

Regardless of the size of the structure or its use, there can be no denying that there is a global movement going on involving shipping containers. With thousands and thousands of these containers laying at ports around the world and their compact geometric design, it is no wonder that architects and perspective homeowners look at these steel boxes as potential building blocks for their construction projects.

But Why?

The aesthetic appeal of shipping containers cannot be overlooked. The boxy structure lends itself well to contemporary and modern architecture. They can be painted any color that the owner chooses and many owners decide to visually enhance their shape with bright, eye-catching colors. Steel beams and other modern design elements complete the thoroughly edgy, modern look.

Surprisingly, the containers can also be used in architecture that blends well with nature, or the very foundation of the structure may be completely concealed. Subdued colors, exterior finishes or features may hide the true origins for some shipping container homes and buildings.

Shipping containers also appeal to the people that are budget conscious. Depending on the size and complexity of the design, shipping containers can be a wise choice for a home, a vacation house, a guest house, a garage or outbuilding; it is possible to save thousands of dollars by using containers as the basis for construction since they are already self-contained structures.

Since shipping container homes are very trendy, they also have a decided cool factor. It cannot be denied that this style architecture appeals to many people for its edgy, industrial look and the unexpected use of a container for a home in a tranquil mountain forest or seaside setting is very cool. Images of colorful surf shacks or Frank Lloyd Wright-inspired modern architecture lend even more trendiness to this already avant-garde style of architecture.

Fad or Functional?

It has now been over thirty years since the first shipping container house came into being. They have grown from an architectural experiment through the curiosity and oddity stage and now have emerged as an accepted form of contemporary construction. Architects compete in competitions to design edifices using containers, and designers all over the world adore them for their versatility and mobility. They are ideally suited for every type of construction from tiny houses to multilevel hotels.

Shipping container construction has now become its own independent trend. Sharing much of the same culture, advantages, and challenges as tiny houses, shipping containers homes also have their own unique aesthetic, appeal, advantages and drawbacks. In the past thirty years, this contemporary construction style has grown into something completely new and progress is made every day toward more acceptance of shipping container homes as a viable option for residential housing.

We're hearing so much about them that it can be difficult to decide whether the trend is something you should jump on or whether this is the parachute pants of our time which will be looked back upon as nothing but a fashion disaster.

Chapter 2 - The Shipping Container Pros and Cons

The are many advantages of using shipping containers to construct a home. Shipping containers are versatile, durable and are ecologically responsible. In this list, you will discover some of the reasons that shipping containers are enjoying a surge in popularity as building blocks for contemporary architecture:

1. They are a perfect building material. They can be stacked, moved, cut, and molded into any type of home, building or office that you may have in mind. They are equally at home at the beach, in the woods, or in a crowded metropolitan area.

2. Additions are easy. It is not difficult to add on a to a house made of shipping containers. Due to the modular nature of their design and the standardized sizing, houses constructed from shipping containers can be modified or expanded using more shipping containers.

3. They are stackable. You can have a two story home at a relatively inexpensive cost due to the stackable nature of these containers. They can be stacked, or placed side by side. You can even set them perpendicular. The possibilities are endless.

4. They can be transported or moved. Shipping containers are designed to transport goods across oceans on ships and then from the ships to be transported by land on flatbed trucks. Due to their design and size specifications, shipping containers can be constructed and then transported to a building site or moved from location to location far more easily than a traditional house.

5. They have aesthetic appeal. Some people enjoy the contemporary and modern appearance of shipping container architecture and the houses constructed from shipping containers have clean lines and a sleek look. Depending on how you complete your shipping container house, they can appear to be

traditional, or they can be painted eye-catching colors that really emphasize their geometric shape.

6. Shipping containers are inexpensive. The price of an average shipping container is $1000 - $5000 per container. Depending on how you customize your shipping container and the type of house that you are building, this can lead to substantial savings.

7. They are incredibly durable. They are designed to protect goods and cargo on long ocean voyages. They are even waterproof. The durability of their construction means that they have the potential to last decades as a residence with a little bit of routine maintenance.

8. They are strong. Shipping containers are made out of galvanized steel and are stronger than wood construction.

9. They are resistant. Termites and mold may be concerns in traditional home construction, but not when you build your house from shipping

containers. Containers are also incredibly resistant to fire.

10.   Shipping container homes can be built in a short period of time. One of the greatest advantages of shipping container construction is the relatively short period of time that it takes to convert one into a habitable home. Whether you are working by yourself or have a team of contractors, you will find that construction time is greatly reduced. Depending on the complexity of the design and the creature comforts that you would like to install, a shipping container can be converted into a home in as little as three days.

11.   Shipping container construction is good for the environment. Upcycling shipping containers is a fantastic use of shipping containers that would otherwise be rusting at ports all over the world or would have to be melted down at a considerable expenditure of energy.

Why Use Containers?

Despite there being a lot of issues with using the containers there are also plenty of reasons why you should use them as well.

12.　The idea of using a prefabricated structure can save on construction costs. These boxes are already the right shape and size, especially if you only plan on using only one. Buying a readily shaped container is a cost effective choice over having to build from scratch using conventional building methods.

13.　There are thousands of containers across the world literally standing and rusting away because they are no longer useful to the shipping industry. This is poor for the environment and a waste. Socially wastefulness isn't selling anymore. It's eco-friendly because it's upcycling.

14.　These abandoned containers are also a problem because they take up space. Lots and lots of space in fact. There are literally miles of them stacked up since it isn't cost effective for companies to ship them empty they just wait until more cargo needs to go in which leads them to pile up in countries that import more than they export.

15.   Shipping containers are very durable. They're mean to withstand sea, sun, and travel which means they will last a long time. They're strong and have a good structure for building projects.

16.   They're a convenient shape for stacking. Just like building blocks shipping containers are life sized to be stacked. Modular concepts are easy to build on from and these are ideal for modular building.

17.   Their ready-made shape also means that they're quick to build with once delivered since they are ready made and just need modification.

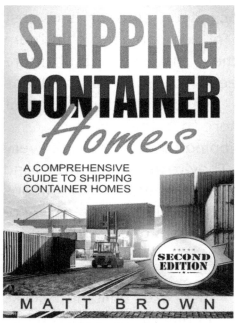

Check out this book!

Preview of Shipping Container Homes
An Essential Guide to Shipping Container Homes with Examples and Ideas of Designs

Introduction

Chances are you've seen them on the road or on a freighter pulling into the port – but did you ever imagine that one of those shipping containers would one day make a home for someone?

Yes, it's true.

Shipping containers have a range of names, such as:

- Steel container
- Cargo container
- International Standards Organization Container – ISO, for short

Whatever you call it, we can all agree that a shipping container seems to be an unusual use for a home – or is it? Whether you live in European countries such as Poland, Norway or Spain, or even across the globe in locations such as the United States, New Zealand, China and South America, shipping container homes are cropping up in a number of housing developments.

Before you brush off the idea, let's go over a brief history and use for these unique boxes and see how they can actually be beneficial for your wallet and the environment!

Chapter 1 – Seriously: A Shipping Container Home?

Why is the interest in transforming shipping containers into homes a growing concept? Though we will get into the benefits and drawbacks in a moment, the main reasons for the growing trend include:

- They're environmentally friendly
- Affordable – nearly half the cost of a traditional home
- Can be customized for any lifestyle

Think shipping container homes is a completely new trend? Not really – early concepts of container living date back to at least 2004 and has picked up steadily since 2010. As the idea of minimizing and going "back to basics" grows worldwide, consumers are looking for more affordable and non-traditional ways to live.

Shopping for a shipping container isn't as easy as one might think, so be ready to dedicate some time and research into finding the right option for you and your lifestyle. A wide range of designs and options exist, all of which come with their own respective benefits and drawbacks. Of course, once you purchase your shipping container, there's more work to be done to transform it into a livable home!

In order to understand more about shipping container homes, it's a good idea to describe some of the basic options and design features. A number of containers are available, but not all of them are conducive to living – which is why research is important before you get started. Understanding key words will help the shopping process go much smoother.

- Tank containers – These cylindrical containers typically carry liquid materials and are mounted on a steel base.

- Dry freight containers – Cubed in shape, these containers open up only with front-facing doors. The opposite end is sealed completely shut.
- Open-top containers – Mostly used for materials such as sand or grain, these containers open up from the top and even sides for greater ease in shipping needs.
- Thermal containers – Used to ship frozen or temperature-sensitive products or materials, but the container itself provides insulation, not refrigeration.
- Refrigeration containers – Commonly known as reefer containers, these shipping containers feature a built-in refrigeration system to keep products or materials cold during transit. Refrigeration containers typically only transport perishable goods.

Global Trends

As one of the more innovative ways to build and design homes, shipping container homes is a growing trend, and there are no signs that such a trend is stopping. Why would people choose to live in a shipping container? There are a number of reasons, the predominant benefits being that they are easily sustained, affordable and provide consumers with a modern, compact look.

They work well in high-population urban areas, as well as off-the-grid homes surrounded by limited resources and conveniences! This diversity in housing attracts potential homeowners from all walks of life.

Continue Reading...

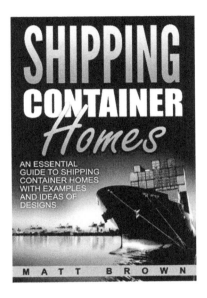

Check out all books by Matt Brown.